William White

A Jubilee Memorial of the Consecration of Christ Church, Cambridge,

which took place June 27th, 1839. To which is prefixed a short history of

Barnwell Priory, from its foundation to the present time

William White

A Jubilee Memorial of the Consecration of Christ Church, Cambridge,
which took place June 27th, 1839. To which is prefixed a short history of Barnwell Priory, from its foundation to the present time

ISBN/EAN: 9783337263003

Printed in Europe, USA, Canada, Australia, Japan

Cover: Foto ©ninafisch / pixelio.de

More available books at **www.hansebooks.com**

A JUBILEE MEMORIAL

OF THE

CONSECRATION

OF

Christ Church, Cambridge,

Which took place June 27th, 1839.

TO WHICH IS PREFIXED

A SHORT HISTORY OF BARNWELL PRIORY,

From its Foundation to the present Time.

BY

WILLIAM WHITE,

Sub-Librarian of Trinity College.

Cambridge:
W. HEFFER, FITZROY STREET.
1889.

TO THE

RIGHT REVEREND CHARLES PERRY, D.D.,

LATE LORD BISHOP OF MELBOURNE,

FORMERLY PATRON OF CHRIST CHURCH,

THIS "JUBILEE MEMORIAL"

IS MOST RESPECTFULLY DEDICATED

BY

THE AUTHOR.

Preface.

ON the 27th of June, 1839, Dr. Allen, Bishop of Ely, consecrated the building since known as Christ Church. Fifty years have now elapsed since that time, and it has been deemed fit that arrangements should be made for the due commemoration of that interesting event. Special Jubilee Services have therefore been fixed for the week in which the anniversary occurs, all the surviving former Vicars have been invited, and the following have accepted the invitation, and will preach on successive evenings:

Monday, June 24, Rev. G. W. Weldon, M.A.

Tuesday, June 25, Rev. Chancellor Leeke, M.A.

Wednesday, June 26, Rev. H. Trotter, M.A.

Thursday, June 27, Rev. A. Delmé Radcliffe, M.A.

Friday, June 28, Rev. C. C. Frost, M.A., formerly Curate.

Sunday, June 30, Rev. J. G. Dixon, M.A., the present Vicar.

As an additional way of marking the Jubilee of Christ Church, it was thought desirable, at a Meeting of the Wardens and Synodsmen, at which the Vicar presided, that a short Memorial of the Church and its doings should be compiled. It was at first intended that this "Jubilee Memorial" should embrace only the space of the fifty years since the consecration of Christ Church; but upon further consideration it was thought that a short history of the Parish of Barnwell from the Foundation of the Priory, however brief, would prove interesting to many who could not easily obtain access to works where only such information is to be obtained; also that it would shew the continuity of church

work in the parish from the Foundation of
the Priory to the present time.

It would only be right here to mention some
of the works which have been consulted in
compiling this "Memorial."

> Dugdale's *Monasticon Anglicanum.*
> *Bibliotheca Topographia Britannica*, Vol. V., which
> contains Rutherforth's Abstract of the Register
> of Barnwell Abbey.
> Cooper's *Annals.*
> ,, *Memorials of Cambridge*, Vol. III.
> *Some Account of Barnwell Priory*, by Marmaduke
> Pricket.
> *The History of Jesus Lane Sunday School.*
> *Memoir of the Right Rev. Bp. Titcomb*, by the Rev.
> Allen T. Edwards.
> &c. &c.

An answer to the question which has been
so frequently asked, "Why should we have a
Jubilee?" will be found in the accounts here
given of the awful depths of sin and open
immorality into which the parish had sunk at
the time of the consecration, and the improved
condition of the same at the present time, which

cannot better be described than in the words of Chancellor Leeke, in his Introduction to a History of Jesus Lane Sunday School in 1877: "I question if there is a large poor town parish in the land where there is more real and earnest Christian life than in Barnwell." Is not this a cause for a Jubilee—a time of rejoicing?

It is hoped that this "Memorial" may help many to join with the Psalmist in saying, "I will praise Thee, O Lord, with my whole heart; I will shew forth all Thy marvellous works," for "The Lord hath done great things for us, whereof we are glad."

It only remains to thank those friends who have kindly rendered assistance in compiling this "Memorial"; more especially the former Vicars, who have given much information concerning the parish during the time of their respective residences in it.

W. W.

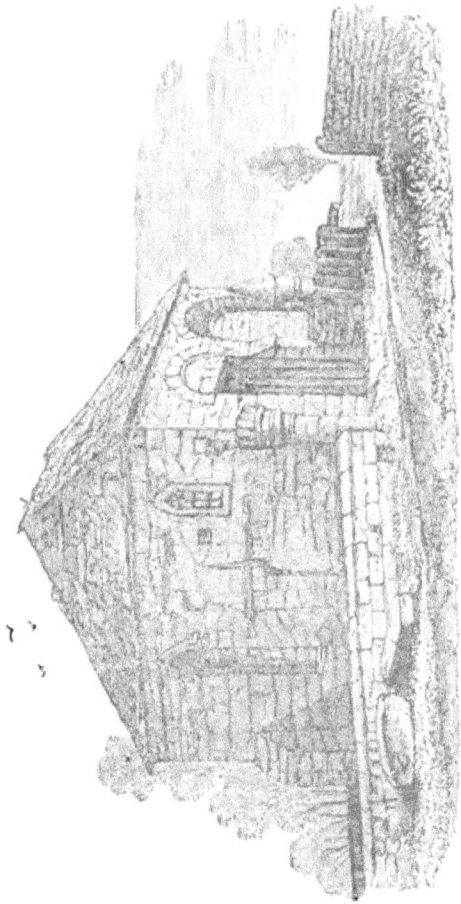

The Remains of Barnwell Priory.

The Priory of Barnwell.

WILLIAM THE CONQUEROR bestowed upon Picot, a Norman, the very rich Barony of Bourn in Cambridgeshire. This Baron was sheriff of Cambridge in or about the year 1092, where his wife, whose name was Hugoline, was taken so seriously ill that she was given over by the physicians; upon which she is said to have made a vow to God and St. Giles, her patron saint, that if she recovered her health she would build a church, and establish a house of religion. To this vow her husband consented. Upon her recovery they built a church to the honour of St. Giles, with convenient apartments, in which they placed six canons regular, under the superintendence of Geoffrey, canon of Huntingdon ; to which they gave, for their maintenance, two parts of the tythes of all their demesnes, and of the demesnes of all their knights pertaining

B

to the Barony of Bourn in Cambridgeshire. They
gave them also the advowson of all the churches
which belonged to them.

Before the convent was complete, both Picot and
his wife died; leaving their estates and honours
to their son Robert, whom they charged to finish
that work. But he, in the reign of Henry I., being
charged with conspiracy, fled; his estate and barony
were confiscated; and the convent of St. Giles was
reduced to very great want and misery. In process
of time Henry I. gave the barony, together with the
site where Barnwell Abbey was afterwards built, to
Payn Peverel, who upon coming to Cambridge, and
seeing the house of St. Giles desolate, said, that as
he had succeeded to the possessions of Picot, so he
would succeed him in finishing the work which he had
left imperfect. But not liking the position of the
Convent of St. Giles, more especially as they had not
the conveniency of a spring, he resolved upon removing
it to a more pleasant situation on the other side of
the river, to a place called Barnewelle, a corruption
of Beorna-wylla, or the Spring of the Children; on this
spot Godilo, a pious Saxon, had established a hermitage
and built a little oratory of wood to the honour of
St. Andrew the Apostle; but he dying, had left the
place without inhabitant, and his oratory without a
keeper. Here Payn Peverel erected a new habitation
for the canons, which was much more commodious
than the old one, in which he resolved to place thirty
canons, under the former Prior, Geoffrey. In 1112 the
canons removed to their new monastery. Payn Peverel

also commenced building a church of wonderful beauty and solidity, but before he had completed all he intended doing, he died of a fever in London, in the 10th year (1122) after the translation of the canons to Barnwell; to which place his remains were brought, and buried on the north side of the great altar in the Priory Church.

His son, William, who succeeded him, confirmed to the canons all the donations of his father, and also gave them a hide of land in Bourn. Afterwards he went to Jerusalem, and died there, leaving his four sisters his co-heiresses. One of these marrying Hamo Peche, the patronage of Barnwell Priory came into that family. Geoffrey died at a great age, and was succeeded by Gerard. The Church lay unfinished the latter part of his time, as also that of his two successors, Richard Noel and Hugh Domesman, who gave large possessions to the Priory.

Robert, surnamed Joel, who was made Prior in 1135, having prevailed upon Everard de Beche, a famous knight, to give him both assistance and advice for the building of offices and re-building the church, took up the very foundations of the church which had been begun by Payn Peverel, and built a more decent and commodious one in its stead, which was dedicated to the honour of St. Andrew and St. Giles on the 11th of May, 1191.

King John gave the Prior and Convent £10 in silver; and on the 27th of April, 1199, he granted them the town of Chesterton in fee farm. He also granted them a fair at Barnwell, commencing on Midsummer eve. He appears to have been at Barnwell on the 17th of March, 1200.

Gilbert Peche caused the remains of his great grandfather, Hamo Peche, and Alice, his wife, to be disinterred, and buried in a marble tomb on the north side of the great altar of the Priory Church. He was a considerable benefactor to the Priory; amongst other things, he gave to this house the perpetual advowson of the Church of St. George in Barnwell; and granted the canons, by deed dated at Barnwell the first Sunday in Advent, 1256, free leave to elect a Prior, reserving to himself and his heirs merely the right of confirmation, and a limited right of taking possession during a vacancy.

It appears that the Church of St. Giles, which had been built by Picot and attached to the Priory, had been lost by the Prior and Convent of Barnwell, for at Prior Robert's earnest importunity, William, Bishop of Ely, restored it to them, when it was assigned for defraying the charge for curing the sick canons and bleeding those who were in health.

A hospital for lepers, called St. Mary Magdalene Hospital, Sturbridge, was established in this parish before 1199, at which date the lepers recovered in the King's Court a free tenement in Comberton. To this Hospital King John granted in 1211 a Fair, in the close of the said Hospital, on the Vigil and Feast of the Holy Cross (13th and 14th of September). From this grant is supposed to have originated the famous Fair called Sturbridge Fair.

During the Priorates of William Devoniensis,

William de Bedford, and Richard de Burgh very little
progress appears to have been made in the buildings of
the monastery; but in the Priorate of Lawrence de
Stanesfeld, a considerable effort was made towards
their completion. In his time the following buildings
were erected : the chapel of St. Edmund, the refectory,
the great hall for guests, the granary, the bake-house,
the brew-house, the stables, the walls, the inner and
outer gates and the barns. He died at an advanced
age, and was buried at the entrance to the chapel of
St. Mary. Nothing appears to have been done by
Henry de Eya, but Johan de Thorleye added a hand-
some appartment to the Prior's Lodge, a private chapel,
and part of the west side of the cloister.

In the Civil Wars between King Henry and his
Barons, the adherents of the insurgent barons com-
mitted great excesses at the Priory, and would have
burned down this house but for the intercession of
Sir Hugh Peche and his brother.

In the evening of February 3, 1287-8, a great tempest
arose, when a terrible flash of lightning struck the
Cross on the summit of the Tower of the Priory
Church, which not only destroyed the Tower, but set
fire also to the Choir, and did great damage to the
windows and other parts of the building. The wind
being very high, caused the sparks to fly upon the
neighbouring houses, and set fire to them. The fire
raged all that night and the next day. Through the
exertions of Robert de Hekitone, sacrist of the Church,
the repairs were almost completed in two years.
John de Kyrkebi, Bishop of Ely, performed the

ceremony of reconciling the Church in March, 1288.
From the fire to the latter date service was performed
in St. Mary's Chapel.

Edward II. was at the Priory the 18th, 19th and
20th of February, 1325-6.

September 9th, 1388, Richard II. held a Parliament
at Barnwell Priory. Here it was that the King delivered
all the temporalities of the Bishopric of Ely to John
Fordham, whom he had preferred to that See. In
this Parliament, John Holland, the King's maternal
brother, was created Earl of Huntingdon. On the
29th of October, 1436, writs were issued by Henry VI.
convening a Parliament at Cambridge on the 21st of
January, 1436-7, but the place of meeting was changed
to Westminster; also on the 14th of December, 1446,
but the place was again changed to Bury St. Edmunds.
During the king's residence at the Priory, 16th of
October, 1438, he extended the duration of Midsummer
Fair.

Edward IV. was at Cambridge in 1463, and the
Queen in 1468.

John Willyamson was charged with having stolen
on the 18th of April, 1475, two silver gilt chalices from
the old Church of St. Andrew, Barnwell.

Synods of the diocese were frequently held in the
conventual Church. At one of them John Alcock,
Bishop of Ely, delivered a discourse, which he caused to
be printed with a curious punning title. In another
Synod held here, 9th July, 1528, the celebration of mass
in "rugged gownes" was prohibited, and Rectors and
Curates were forbidden to use the new translation

of the Bible. About the close of 1529, Nicholas
West, Bishop of Ely, preached in the Church of this
Priory against Hugh Latimer, whose sermons in behalf
of the Reformation were then causing much con-
troversy.

Prior Nicholas Smith not agreeing with King
Henry VIII's measures was compelled, in 1534, to resign
his office, as appears by the following record, which
being very characteristic of the King, may prove
interesting. It is extracted and translated from Bishop
Goodrich of Ely's Register :

"Henry the Eighth, by the Grace of God of
"England and France King, Defender of the
"Faith, Lord of Ireland, and of the Church of
"England, as well by the authority of the Synod
"as the Parliament Supreme Head, to the
"Reverend Father in Christ, Thomas, by Divine
"permission Bishop of Ely, greeting : Know
"that to the election lately made in our Monastery
"or Priory of Barnwell, in your diocese,—whereby
"that wary and discreet man Master John Badcock,
"formerly Canon of the same place, was elected to
"the office of Prior, vacant by the free resigna-
"tion of Master Nicholas Smith, last Prior of
"that place, made into our hands and accepted
"by our authority,—we have granted our royal
"assent and favour : Wherefore we command
"you, by these presents, to confirm, ratify, and
"approve of this election by your authority in
"the usual form ; otherwise we shall take care to
"supply the defect arising from your preceding

"negligence, by our authority as supreme head of
"the aforesaid church.—In witness whereof we
"have caused these our letters patent to be issued.
"Witness my hand at Westminster, this 24th of
"November, in the 26th year of our reign. By
"writ under our private seal, and the aforesaid
"authority of Parliament.

Crumwell."

By virtue of the above patent John Badcock was
constituted Prior of Barnwell, and presented on the
24th of November, 1534, and continued in that office
till the dissolution, when he surrendered the Monastery
on the 8th of November, 1539, to Henry VIII., by
whom it was dissolved; Badcock obtaining a Pension
of £6 per annum. He was the last Prior of Barnwell.
After the dissolution of his Monastery, and the death
of John Lacy and his Wife (who had taken a lease
of the lands and tythes belonging to the dissolved
Priory in Cambridge and Barnwell, of King Henry VIII),
Badcock took the said lease and farmed the lands
and tythes. He appears to have continued his services
in this Church for many years as its Rector. He died
in 1562.

By an Inquisition in the Reign of Edward I. it
appeared that Sturbridge Fair was granted by King
John to the Hospital of Lepers for the use and sub-
sistence of the Lepers dwelling therein. The Perpetual
Curate of St. Andrew the Less had usually been
appointed to the Office of Preacher at this Fair, but
in 1710, a dispute arose between the Corporation of
Cambridge and the Patron of Barnwell respecting the

right of appointing such Preacher. The Mayor appointed a Preacher ; the Patron and Minister protested
against such appointment. Eventually the Minister
of Barnwell gave notice to the people at the Fair that
the Services would, in future, be held in the Church,
and thus ended this mighty dispute.

The Village of Barnwell.

THE Village of Barnwell, after the dissolution of the Priory, can scarcely be said to have had a history, so small was the place. In 1728, there were only 181 persons in the parish, which is about 10 miles in circumference; and on the 30th of September 1731, the whole place, except the Church and six houses, was destroyed by fire. In 1794, there were 320 inhabitants, which number, from some unascertained cause, again fell in 1801 to 225. August 14, 1807, the Royal assent was given to an Act for inclosing the lands of this parish, which was greatly opposed at the time; but it will be seen by reference to the accompanying table, extracted from the Parliamentary Returns to the Population Act, that the parish has from that period gone on increasing with rapid strides:

Year.	Houses.				Persons.		
	In-habited.	Unin-habited	Build-ing.	By how many Families occupied.	Males.	Females.	Total.
1801	79	..	..	79	165	87	252
1811	95	1	7	102	194	217	411
1821	385	9	37	393	1062	1149	2211
1831	1419	83	16	1493	3235	3416	6651
1841	1953	260	21		4552	4934	9486
1851	2365	130	5		5624	6152	11776
1861	2553	137	7		5583	6265	11848
1871	3390	97	58		7610	8348	15958
1881	4342	124	89		7610	9900	21078

It should be known that the present Church,
commonly called the Abbey Church, was never a portion
of the before-mentioned Barnwell Priory Church.
That was of very large dimensions—said to have been
one of the largest in England—and very magnificent.
It contained several chapels; we find mention of the
Chapels of St. Peter, St. Mary and St. Edmund, and
St. Hugh. The first notice of the so-called Abbey
Church occurs in the Taxation of Pope Nicholas in
1291; there it is called "Capella de Bernewelle,"
the Chapel of Barnwell; and the Prior of Barnwell
is stated to be the Rector thereof, which would not

have been the case had it been a portion of the
Priory Church. The style of the architecture (Early
English) agrees with this period. It seems, therefore,
very probable that this Chapel was built for the special

use of the people of the village of Barnwell, and was
served by the Prior, as Rector, or one of his canons.
That may also account for its being left intact, whilst
the very foundations of the Priory itself have been
dug up and carted away. When the site of the Priory
was dug over in 1812, a vast number of slender pillars
of Purbeck marble were found, which would indicate
that in that portion of the Priory Church the Early
English style of architecture prevailed. Perhaps this
might have been the Lady Chapel, built about 1220.
Only one small portion · probably a part of the
Refectory—is at present left to speak of the style and

former splendour of the Priory. It has plain lancet windows and a very good vaulted roof. This building and a piece of land surrounding it has been most generously given by Mr. Joseph Sturton, of Cambridge, to the Cambridge Antiquarian Society.

Edward VI. granted the monastic estate and rectorial tythes to Edward Lord Clinton, and in the 14th year of Queen Elizabeth the same property was in the hands of Thomas Wendy, Esq., son of Dr. Wendy, of Hasling-field, who, according to Masters' History of Corpus Christi College, gave more than 182 loads of stone from the late Priory of Barnwell to Bene't College to build their Chapel (which is now the College Kitchen). It is thought that we may date the destruction of the Priory from this period. How long the Barnwell Priory Estate remained in the possession of Mr. Wendy's family is not certain, but in 1659 it belonged to the family of Chicheley of Wimpole, for in that year Neville Alexander Butler obtained it, in exchange for an estate at Orwell, from Sir Thomas Chicheley. Mr. Butler then came hither to dwell, being the first owner that lived on the estate since the dissolution. The mansion, which bears the date of 1678, was probably erected by him. The estate remained in the possession of the Butler family until the year 1756, when it was sold to Geo. Riste, Esq. In 1763 it was conveyed to Thomas Panton, Esq., under a settlement, made on the marriage, in 1767, of his son, of the same name. The estates ultimately passed to Priscilla Barbara Elizabeth, Baroness Willoughby of Eresby, wife of Peter Lord Gwydir, and the Hon. Peter Robert

Drummond Burrell, their son, by whom it was sold in 1813 to Dr. Geldart. Soon after Dr. Geldart came into possession of the estate he built a church on the ground now occupied by the Mill Road Cemetery. But this, not long after the consecration of Christ Church, was pulled down. The Rev. Geo. Fisk, of Corpus Christi College, used to preach at this Church.

The Abbey grounds were in 1886 purchased from the Geldart family by Mr. Sturton, before referred to, who has since made roads through the estate, and sold most of the land in small building lots. It is now fast being covered with houses.

About the year 1825 the Abbey Church appears to have been allowed to fall sadly into decay, as on the 9th of February of that year the Court of King's Bench discharged a Rule obtained by the Rev. Dr. Geldart and others, calling on the Churchwardens of St. Andrew the Less to shew cause why a Writ of Mandamus should not issue commanding them to repair the Church of that parish. In 1846, the structure had become so dilapidated that it was obliged to be closed as unfit for Divine Service. And an Instrument was executed by the Church Building Commissioners, the Bishop of Ely, the Patron, and the Incumbent, bearing date 26 January, 1846, making Christ Church the Church of the Parish to all intents and purposes. In 1854, the work of restoration was undertaken by the Cambridge Architectural Society, and carried out with much propriety. The Incorporated Society for Building Churches contributed £130 towards its restoration.

As Sunday Schools form an important factor in the

solution of the difficult problem of successful parochial organization, we may usefully relate the history of their development in connection with Barnwell Parish.

On a Sunday morning, early in the Spring of 1827, a party of undergraduates were discussing the question as to the most profitable use of their Sunday leisure. One of them suggested that a part of their time might be given to the religious instruction of such young children as they might be able to gather together for that purpose. The sadly neglected condition of Barnwell was pointed out, and the place as offering a suitable field of work. After further deliberation, it was resolved that a suitable room be secured in Cambridge, to which the Barnwell children should be invited, and a canvass of that parish be made at once by Messrs. J. M. Brown, A. W. Brown, W. Leeke (the father of the present Chancellor Leeke), A. T. Carr, and J. W. Harden. The efforts of these gentlemen were singularly successful, and no less than 220 scholars were gathered together in the Meeting House belonging to the Society of Friends, under the charge of 20 gownsmen as teachers, who were assisted by the wives of some Fellow Commoners. Thus was commenced that organization of world-wide fame, which (owing to the situation of the Friends' Meeting House in that locality) has ever since been known as the "Jesus Lane Sunday School." It was not to be wondered at that Barnwell should have been selected as the place most in need of help, for the dissolute and heathenish condition of the inhabitants at that time was openly notorious. It is to be feared that the bad name which was then, not undeservedly, applied to Barnwell has not yet been dissociated from the place, although the earnest christian effort which has been expended for its benefit shows such wonderfully good results.

In the year 1833 the Committee of Management found that the accommodation afforded by the Friends' Meeting House was insufficient for the increasing number of children in attendance. Arrangements were made with the Governors of the Old Schools for the transfer of the enterprise to the building in King Street, then occupied as an Elementary Day School. Here the work was carried on with uninterrupted success for many years. In this School a considerable number of future rulers in Church and State, as well as a numerous company of parochial clergymen, obtained an excellent insight into an important branch of religious and philanthropic work.

In 1865 E. T. Leeke, B.A., of Trinity College, became Superintendent, when the question of better accommodation was again mooted. It was finally agreed to erect School Rooms for the special use of this unique organization. The work was at once undertaken, and on October 31, 1867, the New Building situated in Paradise Street was opened, and with the increased accommodation has afforded scope for many different kinds of work. Within its walls are carried on a Higher Grade Boys' School (originated by Mr. Leeke), which educates about 250 boys; a dozen or more Bible Classes; together with a valuable and prosperous Institute, which provides for lads and young men an admirable series of Educational Classes—concerning

which a few words must be added. There was about
this time a pretty general feeling among the Superintendent and Bible Class Teachers of this School
that there was a want of some means of seeing the
elder members oftener, so as to know each other better,
and help one another forward. So the YOUTHS' CLUB,
or, as it is now called, the ALBERT INSTITUTE, was
established by A. E. Humphreys, M.A., Fellow of
Trinity College, and Superintendent of the Jesus Lane
Sunday School, in January, 1872, and has flourished
very vigorously with 150 members annually ever since.
The object of the Club may be defined as the religious,
intellectual, moral and social improvement of working
lads, chiefly those employed in offices, warehouses and
shops. The means adopted to effect this object being
(1) a reading room; (2) a lending library, furnished
with books that youths *will* read and find interesting;
(3) educational classes; (4) fortnightly lectures; (5) brass
and flute bands, hand-bell company and glee society;
(6) cricket and rowing clubs, with athletics and
swimming in the summer season.

The educational classes, five years after its establish-
ment, comprised drawing, reading, writing, dictation,
arithmetic, French, Latin, shorthand, English history,
electricity, elocution, and divinity. Prizes for Bible
questions, essays, chess and draught tournaments, &c.,
were also given.

Many similar Clubs and Institutes have since been
founded on its model by University teachers who have
worked in it.

When the new Schoolrooms were opened, an animated

discussion was carried on at the Teachers' Conference as to "the advisability of having Special Sunday Services for children"; but it was not till 1872 that the Superintendent (Mr. Humphreys) announced that it was contemplated to build a Children's Church in Wellington Street. This was set about with a will. Collections from the University and town were energetically made and the required sum of £1200 raised. The Bishop of Ely (Dr. Harold Browne) laid the Memorial Stone, and gave a plain and earnest address to a large audience gathered in the street. The Church, dedicated to St. John, was opened in May, 1873, and is used as a Children's and Mission Church.

The year 1877 was the Fiftieth Anniversary of these Schools; and the Committee held a Jubilee Service, at which most of the Old Superintendents and Teachers were present. The present Teachers appealed to their predecessors to join them in raising some permanent Memorial and Thank-offering for past mercies, the outcome of which appeal was that a Building was raised which serves for Bible-Classes on Sundays, and in the week for the Albert Institute. The Building is of two storeys, affording two large Reading Rooms, three Class Rooms, and a Gymnasium.

The Schools on the East Road were established in 1835. They were built by, and under the management of, the Governors of the Old Schools in Cambridge. The Vicar of the Parish is an ex-officio Governor of these most excellent and beneficial Schools.

In the several transfers of the Priory estate the owner became in right thereof the patron of the parochial church ; but the advowson of the benefice, formerly a donative curacy, was parted with in 1835 by Dr. Geldart to the Rev. Chas. Perry (afterwards Bishop of Melbourne), who became the Patron. Although he threw himself heartily into Evangelistic work in the Parish of Barnwell, he never held the Living, but in 1837 appointed the Rev. Thomas Boodle, M.A., of Trinity College, to the Incumbency.

Christ Church, Barnwell.

THE needs of a growing population, which now numbered between 7000 and 8000 inhabitants, with church accommodation for less than 500, had led to the undertaking of a scheme for the erection of two additional places of worship. The one known as Christ Church was the first built, at a cost of £3800, which, by the energy and zeal of Mr. Perry, was raised by subscription—towards which he contributed £200. The ancient structure, which had for several centuries served the purpose of a parochial church, was at this time in a ruinous condition; and indeed, in 1846, it became necessary to close it altogether, as unfit for Divine service.

Christ Church was opened for service on the 24th of May, 1839, and consecrated by Dr. Allen,

Bishop of Ely, on the 27th of June in the same year. The other Church, St. Paul's, on the Hills' Road, was opened for service on the 17th of May, 1843, and consecrated by the same Bishop on the 15th of October, 1844. The cost of erection was also defrayed by subscription, Mr. Perry giving a like sum (£200) towards it. The architect of both these Churches was Ambrose Poynter, Esq.

The Rev. THOS. BOODLE (who had been for the last two years Incumbent of the Abbey Church) became the first Vicar of Christ Church. He was a hard working, painstaking man, whose heart must often have sunk

within him at the herculean task which lay before him
—the attempt to cope with the enormous amount of
iniquity which was rampant at that time in Barnwell.
He visited much in the Parish, and many and many a
family were blessed by his bright smile and fatherly
advice. He was always ready to rejoice at their prosperity or to sympathize with their distress.

In 1838 the Cambridge Refuge, an Institution for
the reformation of unfortunate women who have
strayed from the path of virtue, was established. It is
principally supported by voluntary contributions.

It appears that Mr. Boodle was for some time non-
resident, but resigned the incumbency at the beginning
of 1845.

On the 18th of February of the same year Mr. Perry
offered the living to the Rev. JONATHAN HOLT TITCOMB,
M.A., St. Peter's College, and in April he was presented
to the Incumbency, Mr. Perry guaranteeing an income
of £150. There was at that time a population of
about 7,000, formed, for the most part, of the most
heterogeneous character. In certain parts of the parish
vice abounded, and it would not be too much to say
that there were localities in which decent persons
would have been ashamed to have been seen. Much
had been done by Battiscombe, Fisk, Boodle, and Lane,
but most of all perhaps by the Teachers of the Jesus
Lane and other Schools, who had laid such firm hold
of the minds of the young. When Mr. Titcomb
began his ministry he found a half-empty church, with
about sixty communicants. Much of his after success
depended on the fact that he never allowed himself to

be distracted by any new plan till he had thoroughly consolidated the object on which he was then engaged. In July he opened Cottage Lectures in four different parts of the parish, thus many, who never entered the House of God, had the Gospel brought to them. A goodly staff of District Visitors, among whom the whole parish was mapped out, was shortly raised. About this time the Church Pastoral Aid Society made him a grant towards a Curate and a Lay Assistant.

The Church was soon filled, and the number of communicants greatly increased. The three Sunday Schools, superintended by undergraduates, were well attended and well manned with teachers.

On the 1st of January, 1846, he began his sermons to children, when he addressed some 500 or 600, which he continued monthly during the whole of his ministry. A Provident Society was opened, two working parties of ladies for the poor were held, and a special effort was made for the female outcasts of the parish; by February the number of communicants had increased to 130.

As far as outward appearances went there were manifest indications of prosperity, and of a revival of religious interest and life in the parish; but there was one subject which pressed heavily upon his mind—the impossibility of bringing the message of the Gospel to those who never attended church or any means of grace. After much prayer, due consideration and taking advice of friends, he determined upon trying open-air preaching. His plea was based on the following considerations: 1. The Bible authorises it. 2. Eccle-

siastical usage sanctions it. 3. The state of the parish
requires it. 4. Ministerial responsibility demands it.
5. Love for the Church of England invites it. Strong
in his own convictions, he made his first attempt on
13th June, 1851, at the back of New Street. From his
own words we know he had no reason to be cast down
at the result of his first attempt. He says, "It pleased
God to bring to that hallowed spot (for so I must call it)
not less than 2,000 souls......The attention was
beyond my expectation. Many of those rough men,
whom I thought would interrupt me, had tears rolling
down their furrowed cheeks when they heard of their
dear Redeemer's love." This open-air preaching was
extended to many parts of the parish, but he had
hitherto shrunk, on account of its apparent hopelessness,
from the duty of preaching on Midsummer Common
at the time of the Fair. In 1857 he resolved upon
attempting this, and took up his post about 200 yards
from the booths, and preached to large assemblies for
the five nights of the fair.

Early in 1859 Mr. Titcomb accepted the office of
English Secretary to the Christian Vernacular Education
Society. In March he entered upon his new duties,
though he did not finally leave Cambridge till Midsummer. He preached his farewell sermon on the
3rd Sunday in June.

The Rev. CHARLES KIRKBY ROBINSON, M.A., Fellow
of Catharine College, succeeded Mr. Titcomb as Vicar
of St. Andrew the Less. He was Inducted to the Living
in 1859, at which time he found a well-filled church, and
during the time of his residence amongst us he kept

the congregation well together; but after about two
and a half years he resigned the Living, in consequence
of his being elected to the Mastership of his College,
and the church was for about six months without
a pastor.

The Living was then offered to and accepted by the
Rev. GEORGE WARBURTON WELDON, M.A., Trinity
College, Dublin, who has very kindly responded to the
request for information concerning the parish during
his residence in it, by giving a very lucid and interesting
account, which it is thought best to publish in his own
words :—

"Having been requested to give an account of the
condition of the Parish of St. Andrew the Less when
I was appointed to it in the year 1862, the following
summary may be deemed sufficient.

"As to the part acted by myself in the organisation
of the parish I desire to say as little as possible.
Whatever measure of success may have attended the
labours of those who took a prominent part in the
work, humanly speaking, is due to my valued friend—
the Rev. W. J. Beamont, Vicar of St. Michael's and
Senior Fellow of Trinity College. He was the prime
mover in bringing about the success which attended
the work of Church Extension in Barnwell. That this
was so, will be seen from the following facts:

"It would be impossible to exaggerate the low estimate in which certain portions of the parish of Barnwell
was held in the year 1862. Streets rejoicing in the
nomenclature of such illustrious and historical names
as those of Wellington and Nelson were sunk in a very

E.

low state of demoralisation. In these streets there was
not, I believe, a single house that was not the resort
of characters of bad repute. I have witnessed scenes
in these localities, even in open day, that could hardly
be credited. Those places, by a kind of tacit consent,
were abandoned to vice. Nelson Street went by the
name of 'Devil's Row.' These were the worst streets,
but there were other parts of the parish, not perhaps
so notorious, still equally disreputable. There were
a few streets off East Road where Proctorial visits were
matters of almost nightly occurrence. The name of
Barnwell had fallen into such disrepute that, when a
district Post Office had been opened in the street
immediately opposite the Vicarage, a deputation of the
inhabitants waited upon me to request that I should
apply to the Post Office authorities to ask them not
to have the letters from the parish, that passed through
that Post Office, stamped with the name of Barnwell
on the envelope. When I asked why there was so
much objection raised to it, I was told that 'friends
at a distance did not like it to be known that letters
came to them from a place which bore so bad a
character.' Accordingly, I wrote to Mr., afterwards
Sir Andrew Trollope, whose official position in connection with Post Office matters was likely to secure the
desired result. His reply was somewhat characteristic
of the well-known writer. In a serio-comic vein he
good-humouredly referred to the improved tone which
the Church Extension scheme had at the date of his
letters produced in the locality, and he adds, 'in a
purified Barnwell we may hope that the name will ere

long be looked upon as an honourable distinction.'
I do not know that I could state any fact more strikingly
suggestive of the ill-omened repute which the parish
bore at the time of my being appointed to it.   No
wonder that the Trustees had in vain offered the Living
to clergyman after clergyman when the appointment
of the present Master of St. Catharine's to that College
caused a vacancy in the parish of St. Andrew the Less.
Five months and a fortnight had elapsed from the date
of Canon Robinson's resignation, and still no one
could be found willing to accept the responsibility of
the position.   It was at that juncture that I received
a letter from my friend, the Reverend Henry Venn.
He stated that my name had been mentioned to the
Trustees by Canon Hoare, of Tunbridge Wells, and he
also informed me that unless a nomination were made
within a fortnight the appointment would lapse to the
Bishop of the diocese.   He then asked me to call upon
him at the Church Missionary House the following
day.   In the interview which then took place, I must
do Mr. Venn the justice to say that he painted the
parish of Barnwell in the substance and coloring of its
real character.   So much so that he suggested that
I should go down at once and look at the position
before accepting it, lest I should be disappointed.   My
reply was as follows: 'No, I shall not go down.   If
you have no one else, I am ready and willing to accept
the offer, and, until I am actually instituted, I will not
visit the parish.'

"The usual formalities were gone through; and
accordingly, on the 14th February, 1862, my License

was duly made out and signed by the Bishop of Ely.

"The following Sunday I visited the parish Church for the first time, quite unofficially. On my way to the Church before morning service I happened to meet the son of an old friend in the street, an undergraduate of Emmanuel College. When I told him where I was going, and the reason, he was greatly surprised, and said what I cannot easily forget, 'What! going to the parish of Barnwell—you don't mean to say so. Why, it would be better for you to go among the Zulus. You have no idea of the kind of place you are going to. No undergraduate not engaged in parish work could be seen there without the taint of suspicion.'

"Such was the character of Barnwell as it was in 1862, both on the testimony of the inhabitants themselves and the townspeople of Cambridge. In fact, the name of Barnwell was almost a term of reproach, and people used to speak of it with a certain air of apologetic hesitancy.

"My predecessors had done much—very much—for the benefit of the parish, but the increase of the population was out of all proportion to the machinery for parochial organisation such as the exigencies of the case demanded. In 1821 there were 2211 inhabitants in the parish, in 1831 there were 6651, and in 1862 there were close upon 13000. When I was appointed I found only one Curate, and he not a member of the University; the other Curate, the Rev. Henry Collis, left just before I entered upon my duties, so that I found before me only the Curate of the advanced age of sixty years and one Scripture-reader. There was quite a small army of parish workers, who laboured with an intelligence and ability suited to the importance of the demands made upon them by so large a population.

"At that time the church accommodation consisted of Christ Church, capable of holding 1400 persons; the Abbey Church, about 120; and a very little Mission Room in Gas Lane, where services were held by laymen for the benefit of the very poorest of the population in a building not capable of holding more than twenty people. There were three Sunday Schools—the Abbey, Gas Lane, and Jesus Lane, at that time situated in King's Street in an adjoining parish. In these Schools there were between 1700 and 1800 children. About a hundred undergraduates one way or another worked in Term-time in the parish, and out of Term their places were taken by teachers living on the spot. Of lady teachers and district visitors there were between seventy and eighty, exclusive of supernumeraries.

"Such was the condition of Barnwell as I found it. What Barnwell is to-day in the year 1889, one has only to look round in order to form a proper estimate. In 1862 there were men and women living there who had never entered any place of worship. Many had never been baptized. I had a list of names, numbering some hundreds, who, though living together as husbands and wives, had never been married. The place where now stands St. Matthew's Church was the rendezvous of gipsies, cinder-sifters, cadgers, and Bohemians of all kinds, as wild, indeed some of them wilder, than the children of the prairie. Let any one now look at St.

Matthew's Church and its surroundings, and he will find it hard to believe the account I have here given of what the locality was like in the year to which I refer.

"I desire emphatically to give the honour of the great work of successful Missionary labours carried out during my years of office to those who worked with me in the parish. First upon the list I place my friend Beamont. Soon after I went into residence he proposed to me a scheme of Church Extension, which I gladly accepted. The case at this time stood thus. The Church Pastoral Aid Society allowed a grant of £200 a year. The Living was worth only £220 from all sources. By Mr. Beamont's persistent efforts the University granted me £300 a year to procure additional Curates, and after a sermon preached by Dr. Vaughan before the University, some Fellows of their Colleges very generously volunteered their parochial services. Thus, in a little time we had as many as seven Curates, including volunteers and regulars, working in the parish. And this state of things continued with but little intermission up to the time of my resignation in the year 1869. Had it not been for the liberal grant from the University Chest, the work could not have been carried out as successfully as it has been. The Barnwell of to-day is so unlike the Barnwell of a quarter of a century ago that those who do not know its past history can form no adequate idea of the wonderful change that has passed over the place. No one could possibly realise the difference between Gas Lane as it is and Gas Lane as it was, except those who can call to mind the

history of the past. At that time, when the foundations
of St. Matthew's Church were being laid, the site was
strongly objected to, because it was so much out of the
way, and in the very outskirts of the parish. It was
actually in the fields, and not a single house beyond it.
But, look at it now, with a new town built all round
it, and a new population added to old Barnwell, new
schools, new Mission rooms, and all sorts of parochial
machinery in masterly activity. When I visited the
place in 1882, I was so bewildered with the new streets
that I could not easily find my way. It was a pleasant
surprise to me to find that Wellington Row had under-
gone such complete moral fumigation that, owing to
the energy of Canon Leeke, a children's Church had
been built there, and has been since used every Sunday
for Special Services. *Heu mutatus!*

"When the University voted their generous grant,
it occurred to some of us that it might be well to
divide the parish into four districts and to give one
to each of the regular Curates. The districts were
as follows:—

(1) Christ Church, with about 3500 people.
(2) The Abbey Church, with about 3000.
(3) Gas Lane, with about 3000.
(4) East Road district, with about 2500.

"These several districts were worked regularly by
the Clergy specially set apart for them, so that they
were in sole charge as quasi-incumbents.

"With grateful, though in some instances with
sorrowful memory, I call to mind the vanished past—
the days that are no more, and my clerical brethren, my

friends and fellow-labourers, some of whom are gone to their rest and to their reward. Others are settled down in quiet country parishes, or have been elected to positions of useful prominence. To all who still survive, and who may perhaps read these lines, I desire to renew my heartfelt thanks, and to assure them, wherever they are, that neither time nor place have dimmed the recollections of the days that are gone, or of the old associations of parish work in which during those seven years we were so pleasantly and usefully engaged.

"For my own part, all I can say is that, in looking back upon my past experience of parochial work in Barnwell, I have done not what I wished to do exactly, but the best I could under the circumstances, and I heartily wish that it had been better."

It was in Mr. Weldon's time that the Weekly Offertory was established.

Upon the resignation of Mr. Weldon, a successor was found in the person of the Rev. EDWARD TUCKER LEEKE, M.A., Fellow of Trinity College and Superintendent of the Jesus Lane Sunday Schools. He was Instituted by Dr. Edward Harold Browne, Bishop of Ely, at Ely House, London, on the 23rd of June, 1869; Inducted to the Living, in the following week, by the Rev. Dr. Campion of Queens' College, Rural Dean; and read himself in on the morning of Sunday, July 4, 1869.

A Mission was commenced on the 17th of February, 1870, which lasted until the 23rd. The Rev. E. H. McNeile was the principal Missioner, assisted by many Clergy and laymen.

At Mr. Leeke's request, the Churchwardens called a meeting of seat-holders on June 21, 1871, to ascertain their views as to the re-seating of the Church with open benches in lieu of the then shut-up pews. Open oak benches were put in at the South end (the Church standing North and South), facing East and West. The front and the backs of the seats in the galleries were reduced in height; the pulpit removed from the middle of the Church to one side, and the reading desk to the other, a lectern being placed in the position formerly occupied by the pulpit; thus giving the Church the appearance of a House of Prayer rather than that of a Preaching-house. No further steps, however, were taken at that time to re-seat the remaining portion of the Church.

The Communicants' Prayer Union was instituted in October of the same year.

It was in 1872 that some not over respectable houses in Wellington Street were for sale, and were secured for the purpose of building a Children's and Mission Church, which was licensed May 26, 1873, and is still used for that purpose. It has proved a light in a dark place; and has changed, not only the character of the neighbourhood, but also that of the people living in it.

During the week of March 2—9, 1873, a second Mission was held in this parish, the principal Missioners on this occasion being the Rev. T. H. Wilkinson, Rev. H. J. Carter, and Rev. J. S. Jones, assisted as before by many able and willing hands.

Soon after the time of the Mission, a requisition,

signed by a number of young people of both sexes, was sent in to Mr. Leeke, asking for an early celebration of the Holy Communion, as many of them were unable to attend that in the midday service. This being quite in accordance with his own wishes, he consulted a meeting of the members of the Church, the majority of whom agreeing with him the service was commenced, and is still fairly attended.

On the 9th of March, 1873, Bishop Harold Browne held an Ordination in this Church, when two candidates were admitted to the Priesthood and one to the office of Deacon.

Mainly through the kind offices of the present Bishop of Durham the sum granted by the Committee of the Barnwell and Chesterton Curates' Fund was increased, so as to give extra Curates to the rapidly increasing Parish.

Two Schools were added to those already in existence: one in Eden Street (a Higher Grade School for Girls), the other on ground at the back of St. John's Mission Church, in Wellington Street—the latter in 1875.

Upon the Consecration of Dr. Benson to the See of Truro, the Prime Minister offered the Chancellorship of Lincoln Cathedral, together with a Canonry, to Mr. Leeke, who, after some hesitation, agreed to accept the promotion awarded to him. He sent in his resignation at the beginning of October, 1877, and preached his farewell sermon on the 7th of the same month.

The Rev. HENRY TROTTER, M.A., Corpus Christi

College, Cambridge, next succeeded to the Living. He came into residence as soon as the Rev. E. T. Leeke left, in the Autumn of the year, and held the Living until the end of 1883, when he was appointed to the Rectory of Trowbridge, Wilts.

In order to increase the interest of the lay members of the congregation in Church work, the ancient custom of Synod's men was revived, forming a consultative Church Council.

In the early part of the year 1878 work was begun, at the suggestion of Mr. Allnutt, who was Curate at that time, in the neglected district of Rifle Butts Row; then one long row of cottages and a few scattered houses, across the railway on the path to Cherry-hinton. A cottage was rented and accommodated for use for Week-day and Sunday Schools, Mission Services, and Coffee-room. From a small beginning this work expanded. St. Philip's School Church was built and licensed by the Bishop. On the death of Dr. Geldart, Master of Trinity Hall, the property adjacent to Butt's Row was sold for building purposes, and a large population quickly sprang up as houses were built. A piece of land was secured in the centre, St. Philip's Church was taken down and re-erected upon it; and now, we are happy to say, a new and larger church is being built. The work there was carried on by the following gentlemen, who were licensed by the Bishop: Messrs. Daintree, Maxlow, and L. Bomford; while the Hon. Mrs. Sugden, Mrs. Weymouth, and Mrs. L. Bomford materially assisted in the good work.

During the laying of the branch railway from the Barnwell Junction, a strong effort was made to obtain the use of the Leper Church for Divine Service. A commission was appointed by the University, including Dr. Campion, Rural Dean. Unfortunately no practical result followed. Let us hope that some day it may be restored to its proper use.

The Sunday Schools of the parish continued to be well worked, and the annual gatherings, in which the Jesus Lane Sunday School took part, produced the same enthusiasm and entailed the same careful preparation as of yore. At the Centenary of Sunday Schools, which took place in 1880, the St. Andrew the Less contingent held its own and was not surpassed by any other parish.

In January, 1880, a Ten Days' Mission was held by the Rev. W. H. Aitkin at Christ Church, which left lasting blessings behind it. The Mission included the Abbey and St. John's Churches, where other Missioners held Services.

Evangelistic Services were carried on systematically in the open air; and, during the annual Fairs held on Midsummer Common, a large tent was pitched, in which Services were held, and a free breakfast given to the travelling Fair-people and their children.

The work of parochial visitation was ably supplemented by the Staff of District Visitors and Bible-women.

The temperance work in the parish was advanced by the erection of the Coffee Palace on the East Road.

The work of the Industrial Dwellings Company helped forward the cause of morality in providing better houses for the working classes in Cambridge, and St. Andrew the Less parish profited by its operations; and we must not omit the quiet beneficent work of rescue and reform carried on among a class for which at one time the parish was notorious. Many of the worst houses were closed.

The Rev. ARTHUR HENRY DELME RADCLIFFE, M.A., Trinity College, Cambridge, was the next Vicar. He was inducted to the Living by the Archdeacon of Ely in April, 1884. Many alterations and improvements were made during his time.

First we would mention the improvements made in the Church itself. The pews had long been an eyesore to many members of the congregation, and it was thought that the time had arrived when a change might be made acceptably to all. The Vicar, Churchwardens, and Sidesmen therefore formed themselves into a Committee to solicit subscriptions towards re-seating the Church with open benches of pitch-pine. The appeal was liberally responded to, and the work undertaken and successfully carried out by Mr. Leach. A new Altar-cloth, beautifully worked, had but a short time before been subscribed for by the congregation.

About this time one member of the congregation presented an electro-silver alms-dish, made to match the Communion-service; whilst another presented one of brass. This involved the necessity of substituting offertory bags for the boxes which had been so long in use.

A considerable addition was made to the Vicarage house, chiefly by means of a loan of £750 from

Queen Anne's Bounty, by which the house was made roomy and comfortable.

An alteration was made in the constitution of the Parochial Branch of the Church Missionary Society, by which an Annual Parochial Meeting and Sale of Work was held; which, under God's blessing, concentrated the interest, and resulted in the amount raised for the Society being more than double that of former years.

A Branch of the Girls' Friendly Society was formed by Mrs. Delmé Radcliffe, most efficiently assisted by other ladies in the Parish; it numbered about 130 members and 40 candidates. This Society is believed to have been a great blessing to many girls.

There was a large increase in the number of members of the Band of Hope, chiefly owing to the exertions of the Curates and the ladies who helped them.

Also a Brass Band was formed, which is now attached to the Youth's Branch of the Temperance Society.

In consequence of the large increase of the number of houses on the Abbey estate it was thought advisable to take steps towards the enlargement of the Abbey Church, and a Committee was formed and Plans obtained for the purpose of ascertaining how the enlargement could best be carried out without injury to the present edifice.

In December, 1888, Mr. Delmé Ratcliffe accepted the Vicarage of St. John's, Paddington, and preached his farewell sermon, to a very crowded church, on the

last Sunday of February, 1889. He was a man who
won the hearts of his parishioners by his kind and
gentle manners, and great and real was the grief of
many when the news was spread of his departure from
among them.

The Rev. JOHN GILBERT DIXON, M.A., of Gonville
and Caius College, who is the present Vicar, succeeded.
He was inducted to the Living by the Archdeacon of
Ely on the 16th of April, 1889.

It is much to be regretted that on the appointment
of the new Vicar the Committee of the Barnwell and
Chesterton Curates' Fund felt it necessary to reduce
the Grant towards the stipends of the Clerical Staff
of this populous Parish.

Priors, Perpetual Curates, and Vicars.

~~~~~~~~~~~~~~~~~~~~

PRIORS OF BARNWELL.

1092—Geoffrey of Huntingdon. He survived the removal to Barnwell, where he was buried.

1113—Gerard. In his time many apartments were built, and the Church carried on with diligence.

....—Richard Norrell, or Noel, resigned after two years and went to France.

1115—Hugh Domesman, a Canon, Prior twenty years, died of consumption.

1135—Robert Joel, Prior 33 years, buried at Barnwell.

1197—Another Robert occurs.

1207—William Devonienses, died 25 Jan. 1213-14, buried at Barnwell.

1213—William de Bedford, Sacrist, appointed Nov. 2, 1213, died a few days after his instalment, buried at Barnwell.

1214—Richard de Burgh, died soon after election, buried at Barnwell.

1215—Laurence de Stanesfeld, built most of the offices and the Chapel of St. Edmund, died 1252, buried at Barnwell.

1253—Henry de Eye, resigned in the third year of his Priorate, died 1270, buried at Barnwell.

1256—Jolan de Thorleye, resigned 1266, buried at Barnwell.

1266—Simon de Ascellis, M.A. Oxon., resigned 1297, died the same year, buried at Barnwell.

1297—Benedict de Welton, resigned 1316.

1316—Fulk, elected Dec. 3, 1316.

1330—John de Quye, *alias* Oxney, Canon of Ely.

1340—John de Brunne.

1350—Ralph de Norton, received temporalities July 1.

1383—Thomas de Canterbury.

1392—John Bernewelle, *alias* Outlawe.

1408—William Downe, died 1428.

1428—John Chateriz, received temporalities Dec. 3.

1434—John Page, received temporalities March 22, 1434-5.

1441—John Poket, died Aug. 28, 1464, buried at Barnwell.

1464—John Whaddon, resigned Nov. 10, 1474.

1474—William Tebald, or Thibaud. He was Canon in 1454, and Sub-Prior the same year, and till 1474.

1489—John Leveryington, Precentor 1474.

1495—William Rayson, *alias* Cambridge, received temporalities Feb. 14, 1489-90.

1522—Thomas Rawlyn, *alias* Cambridge, Canon regular, was ordained Sub-Deacon 1490, resigned after 1523, but when is doubtful, died 1543.

1527—Nicholas Smith, compelled to resign 1534, was living in 1551.

1534—John Badcock, who was the last Prior of Barnwell, yielded up his Priory Nov. 8, 1539, to Henry VIII., died about 1562.

PERPETUAL CURATES OF ST. ANDREW THE LESS, BARNWELL.

1620—Francis Hobman.

1620—Ralph Rotheram.

1631—John Goldson.

1646—Thomas Tifford.

1649—William Bagley, died 1665.

*　　　　　*　　　　　*

1671—John Moore, D.D., Sidney, Bishop of Norwich, afterwards Bishop of Ely, was Vicar at this date.

*　　　　　*　　　　　*

1709—William Piers.

1714—Robert Alfounder, B.D., Emmanuel College.

1720—William Butler, B.A., Emmanuel College, died at Cliff, Kent, May 22, 1731, aged 36 years.

* * *

1754—Richard Hurd, D.D., Emmanuel College, Bishop of Lichfield, afterwards of Worcester, died May 28, 1808.

1757—Richard Richardson.

1762—Richard Farmer, D.D., afterwards Master of Emmanuel College, died 1797.

1770—Samuel Blackall, B.D., Emmanuel College.

1774—William Bond, M.A., Caius College.

1776—Thomas Sisson, M.A., Emmanuel College.

1782—Thomas Veasey, B.D., St. Peter's College.

1785—John Bullen, M.A., Emmanuel College.

1818—Richard Relhan, *the Botanist*, M.A., Trinity College.

1821—William Pulling, M.A., Sidney Sussex College, a famous Linguist.

1826—James Geldart, LL.D., Trinity Hall.

1837—Thomas Boodle, M.A., Trinity College, who in 1839 became the first Vicar of Christ Church.

VICARS OF CHRIST CHURCH, BARNWELL.

1839-45—Thomas Boodle, M.A., Trinity College, afterwards Vicar of Christ Church, Virginia Waters, Hants.

1845-59—Jonathan Holt Titcomb, D.D., St. Peter's College, afterwards first Bishop of Rangoon, died April 2, 1887.

1859-62—Charles Kirkby Robinson, D.D., Master of St. Catharine's College, and Canon of Norwich.

1862-69—George Warburton Weldon, M.A., Trinity College, Dublin, incorporated M.A. Trinity College, Cambridge, now Vicar of Bickley, Kent.

1869-77—Edward Tucker Leeke, M.A., late Fellow of Trinity College, Cambridge, now Chancellor of Lincoln Cathedral.

1877-84—Henry Trotter, M.A., Corpus Christi College, now Rector of Trowbridge.

1884-89—Arthur Henry Delmé Radcliffe, M.A., Trinity, now Vicar of St. John's, Paddington, London.

1889—John Gilbert Dixon, M.A., Gonville and Caius College, the present Vicar.

List of Churchwardens.

1839-40—Turner, Samuel Austin.
          Rowe, Richard.
1840-41—Turner, Samuel Austin.
          Rowe, Richard.
1841-42—Naylor, Thomas Hacke.
          Smith, William.
1842-43—Naylor, Thomas Hacke.
          Smith, William.
1843-44—Naylor, Thomas Hacke.
          Cooper, Charles Henry.
1844-45—Naylor, Thomas Hacke.
          Rowe, Richard.
1845-46—Naylor, Thomas Hacke.
          Wisdom, John.
1846-47—Naylor, Thomas Hacke.
          Smith, William.
1847-48—Smith, William.
          Apthorpe, William Henry.

1848-49—Anthony, Thomas,
    Rowe, Richard.
1849-50—Rowe, Richard.
    Wisdom, John.
1850-51—Smith, Thomas.
    Coward, Thomas.
1851-52—Smith, Thomas.
    Coward, Thomas.
1852-53—Smith, Thomas.
    Smyth, William Townrow.
1853-54—Waters, William.
    Smyth, William Townrow.
1854-55—Waters, William.
    Smyth, William Townrow.
1855-56—Waters, William.
    Headley, James Ind.
1856-57—Rowe, Richard.
    Headley, James Ind.
1857-58—Rowe, Richard.
    Waters, William.
1858-59—Waters, William.
    Smith, Thomas.
1859-60—Waters, William.
    Smith, Thomas, who died in November,
      1859, and was succeeded by
    Rowe, Richard.
1860-61—Waters, William.
    Rowe, Richard.
1861-62—Waters, William.
    Rowe, Richard.
1862-63—Rowe, Richard.
    Waters, William.

1863-64—Rowe, Richard.
    Webb, John.
1864-65—Webb, John.
    Smith, William Charles.
1865-66—Bailey, Frederick.
    Smith, William Charles.
1866-67—Bailey, Frederick.
    Rowe, Richard Reynolds.
1867-68—Bailey, Frederick.
    Palmer, Robert Berrington.
1868-69—Bailey, Frederick.
    Wisbey, Alfred.
1869-70—Bailey, Frederick.
    Wisbey, Alfred.
1870-71—Wisbey, Alfred.
    Crawley, Young.
1871-72—Crawley, Young.
    White, William.
1872-73—Crawley, Young.
    White, William.
1873-74—Crawley, Young.
    White, William.
1874-75—Webb, John.
    White, William.
1875-76—Webb, John.
    White, William.
1876-77—White, William.
    Burrows, Robert Cresswell.
1877-78—White, William.
    Burrows, Robert Cresswell.
1878-79—Burrows, Robert Cresswell.
    Francis, Joseph.

1879-80—Burrows, Robert Cresswell.
          Francis, Joseph.
1880-81—Bailey, Frederick.
          Francis, Joseph.
1881-82—Bailey, Frederick.
          Coggin, Henry.
1882-83—Fulford, William.
          Todd, John.
1883-84—Fulford, William.
          Todd, John.
1884-85—Fulford, William.
          Todd, John.
1885-86—Fulford, William.
          Todd, John.
1886-87—Fulford, William.
          Todd, John.
1887-88—Fulford, William.
          Todd, John.
1888-89—Fulford, William.
          Todd, John.

METCALFE AND SON, PRINTERS, CAMBRIDGE.

www.ingramcontent.com/pod-product-compliance
Lightning Source LLC
Chambersburg PA
CBHW021635270326
41931CB00008B/1033